Born Survivors of the Holocaust

The Auschwitz Torture and the Last Generation

Written By

Daniel Hofmann

Table of Contents

Introduction

People who claim that the Holocaust was a fabrication are unable to respond to an elderly survivor's question, "If the Holocaust didn't happen, where is my family?"

For those who are too gullible to believe them, this book contains the piercing, moving, and horrifying experiences of those who survived to remember it.

Think about the prisoner who asked his companion why he was praying and was informed that he was thanking God that he was not made like the killers who worked there, or the prisoner who was using the restroom when he was touched by a guy who was hanging above him. "If you enter a pool, you anticipate being wet. Hangings are something you anticipate seeing there. A little kid describes finding a space to hide among the bodies.

As he strolled past captives who seemed to be "in a trance," a GI who freed the Buchenwald detainees claimed it was worse than a dream. The deceased buddy was wearing what seemed to be a white jacket when it should have been blue, and the lady who discovered him was perplexed when she spotted him among the bodies. It seemed white upon closer examination due to the extent of the lice infestation. Cantor "with a magnificent tenor voice" raced to the electric fence to jump to his death when he could take no more. When the five youths who were going to be hung sprang from the stools and hanged themselves, they gave the Germans no chance. Texans believed that the tattooed number on a woman's forearm served as a memento of a great summer camp experience. Jews burned Friday night candles fashioned of margarine and blanket threads as they traveled to Birkenau. Slaves who received tattoos on their wrists instead of their faces or foreheads considered themselves fortunate.

Sisters standing side by side could not identify one another because of their shorn heads. Russian liberators threatened to rape women unless they shut themselves inside, saying, "We freed you, but now you don't want to love us?" A teenage lady describes being restrained as

physicians removed
unidentified body parts for
studies that prevented her
from becoming pregnant.

World War II survivors of
the Nazi concentration
camps recount their
experiences. Their remarks
are proof that monsters
devoid of emotion rendered
innocents barren. There are
reports of men, women, and
children who were
physically and
psychologically altered as a
result of the actions of
rogue Germans within.

These are slaves'
testimony, whose duty it
was to guide innocent
victims into gas chambers
and then burn their bodies.

The Holocaust

The Holocaust was an unparalleled act of comprehensive and organized genocide carried out by Nazi Germany and its allies with the intention of exterminating the Jewish people.

The anti-Semitic, racist, and Nazi ideology served as the main driving force. Nazi Germany implemented a strategy between 1933 and

1941 that stripped Jews of their property rights and rights to vote, followed by the branding and concentration of the Jewish community.

In Germany and a large portion of occupied Europe, this approach was widely endorsed. Following the Soviet Union's invasion in 1941, the Nazis and their allies began the systematic extermination of Jews in large numbers. Nearly six million Jews had been killed by the year 1945.

I therefore lost my mother,
father, and brother in the
span of seven months.
I am the only one who made
it out alive.

These are the horrors that
the Germans did to us, and
they should never be
forgotten. On the other side,
we got our comeuppance
since the survivors,
including me, were able to
build wonderful families.
This serves as both
retaliation and comfort.

By 1945, the majority of
Jews in Europe had passed
away. An almost 2,000-
year-old society that had
been prosperous was no
more.

Dazed, malnourished, and
profoundly heartbroken, the
survivors—one from a town
and two from the host—
gathered what little strength
and humanity they still had
and rebuilt.

They never punished their
tormentors because they
didn't believe that justice

could ever be served after such a crime. Instead, they focused on rebuilding: new families who would always live in the shadow of the dead; new life stories that would always be marred by the scars; and new communities that would always be plagued by the loss.

This Is the Last Generation

THE 77th anniversary of the liberation of Auschwitz Concentration Camp is on January 27, 2022, in NEW YORK. More than a million innocent men, women, and children were slain in this extermination camp in Nazi-occupied Poland.

This day is observed as International Holocaust Remembrance Day each year, which is important to me. I'm Dana Arschin, and without my grandfather, my Poppy, who survived Auschwitz, I wouldn't be here. I make it my job to tell the tales of Holocaust victims out of respect for my heritage and a duty to preserve the memory.

We are examining the effects of the worldwide

epidemic that we are all now experiencing on how Holocaust victims are remembered and commemorated.

Additionally, we'll share with you some amazing tales of fortitude, courage, tenacity, and hope from the final generation of survivors.

They march in a display of unity, step by step. The International March of the Living has brought together tens of thousands of people

each year for more than 30
years in Poland.

The distance between the
infamous Auschwitz I main
gate and Auschwitz II, the
death camp better known as
Birkenau, is around two
miles. In 2018, I took part in
the march and recorded
every step of the way.

Every year in the spring,
this custom has been
postponed for the last two.

The president of the International March of the Living, Phyllis Greenberg Heideman, remarked, "We feel pretty powerless not being able to go to see the places of devastation of so many of our relatives."

Due to travel limitations and COVID safety concerns, the organization's goal to yearly transport tourists to

Auschwitz has been put on hold.

Even though we are seeing new COVID strains this year, the march is scheduled to continue in April. Less than half of the 10,000 individuals who typically attend are anticipated to sign up.

We are present. We remember, and we won't forget. And despite any challenges, we are

determined to visit Poland,
Heideman stated.

The number of survivors is
decreasing every year.
There are barely 300–350
thousand Holocaust
survivors left in the world,
according to the nonprofit
group Claims Conference.

While they are still with us,
this is our last opportunity to
hear these survivors

describe the atrocities firsthand.

We met several incredible Holocaust survivors during this epidemic, and we also had the opportunity to hear about their COVID survival tales and celebrations. Esther Kosiner, a native of Long Island, turned 100 last year.

Kosiner said, "I have kids; that's why I'm still living; my kids are great. She is inspired to continue living each day to the fullest by her children. In 1921, as the globe was beginning to recover from the Spanish Flu epidemic, Kosiner was born in Germany.

Her sister Rosa was murdered in a Nazi concentration camp, but she and her parents managed to escape. The wounds from Kosiner's early life have persisted despite the years that have gone.

It was wonderful when I was a little girl—until Hitler arrived. If we didn't go to the street and shout "Heil Hitler," they would come after us, according to Kosiner.

Lee Fruchtman is a different survivor who has distinct recollections of her past. We met not long after she turned 101, close to her house in Washington Heights. She describes surviving the war in

Germany and making it to the United States aboard a ship.

When they marched through our neighborhood, we hid beneath the bed, Heil Hitler. Fruchtman described the situation as "extremely sad, terribly terrible, and on the boat I was ill for seven days, very sad."

But Lee put forth a lot of
effort, building a family and
a prosperous life for himself
in New York. She still feels
like she has so much life left
to live despite reaching this
great age milestone. She
claims that staying awake
by working keeps her alive.

If ever a person's fortitude
was put to the test, Jack
Holzberg's tale is it. He was
held in a number of Nazi
concentration camps,
including Mauthausen and

Paszów. Murdered were his mother, two siblings, and father. This 90-year-old New Jersey resident beat COVID after a three-week struggle. Jack was standing while several COVID survivors were being brought out of the hospital.

"I made it, I got home, and I'm OK. Thank God I'm here, Holzberg said in May 2020.

Sadly, Jack Holzberg died immediately thereafter, emphasizing how important it is to hear these first-person tales now, while we still have the opportunity.

The "angel of death" was Josef Mengele. He was an infamous Nazi physician who experimented cruelly on captives at Auschwitz. When they were just 11 years old, I talked with twin boys who had survived those tests. Many years

have passed, and they are
coming up now to ensure
that the world never forgets.

He failed to rescue me!
Peter Somogyi screamed,
"He just saved me for
himself.

More than 75 years after
Peter escaped the
Holocaust, emotions are still
strong and horrific pictures
are still fresh in the mind.

When the 88-year-old, who is now residing in Westchester County, New York, arrived in the Auschwitz Concentration Camp in July 1944, he was just 11 years old. The prisoner number A-17454 that was tattooed on his bicep upon arrival is still clearly visible. He also initially met legendary Nazi physician Josef Mengele during that time.

"Mengele appeared and requested twins. My mother first remained silent, then responded twice with "no," and finally three times with "yes." We were immediately kidnapped by two men, and we were unable to say goodbye," stated Peter.

When the twins were pulled aside, Peter, his twin brother Thomas, their 13-year-old sister Alice, and mother Elizabeth were all unwittingly in line for the gas

chambers. Elizabeth and
Alice were never seen
again.